WALTON WELL

CULTURE ART POETRY FICTION SOCIAL JUSTICE

PRESS

STRANGE SIGNATURES

STRANGE SIGNATURES

POEMS

Ramón García

WALTON WELL PRESS
Los Angeles   Oxford

Cover art: Ramón García, "Strange Signatures," 2025.
11 x 14 inches, mixed media on paper.

Design & Typesetting: ash good

Published by Theresia de Vroom
Walton Well Press
Los Angeles | Oxford

Paperback ISBN: 978-1-964295-11-4

Library of Congress Control Number: 2025917967

WALTONWELLPRESS.COM

For Ulises

Contents

MYSTERY PLAYS: A BLUEBEARD CYCLE

BALLADS OF INNER LIFE, OR THE END OF BLUEBEARD

NATURAL EFFIGIES

The land of the Tarahumara is full of signs, shapes and natural effigies which do not seem to be mere products of accident, as if the gods, whose presence here is everywhere felt, had wished to signify their power through these strange signatures in which the human form is hunted down from every side…

—Antonin Artaud, "Concerning A Journey
to the Land of the Tarahumaras"

The Guards

I am a convict. You won't fall behind.
You are my guard. Our fate is therefore one.
 —Marina Tsvetaeva, "Poems for Akhmatova"

Wherever a poet is born
Is a country at war—no country is an exception.
The poet is prisoner, and words afford
Recreational time in the yard.

The Lives of the Poets— the Virgils, the guards—
Guide derelict pilgrimages
Through the soul's Piranesi pastorals.
They scar myths and gods into our flesh,
Tattoos only lovers and prison mates see, understand,
We relocate from one cell to another,
And bars protect and isolate, like stresses and accents.

A poet's path
Is measured by a shared sentence.
With faith, it's a life sentence—to be committed.
Confinement is escape,
While we wait for the guards to smuggle
The Muse's visiting hours,
The *duende's* contraband.
Only the poet is judge.

Juan Gabriel Ascends to Heaven

Scaling the lyrics of an orphaned soul
Singing is a ladder, we are the steps,
You will reach heaven.

You remained the same on both sides of the border.
Everything changed, but your songs carried on
Untouched by the vicissitudes of alienation.

Somehow you were always there….in the blank spots
Of time, a constant, irrefutable
Promise, a sad celebration, emotional carnival…

On the radio, all those childhood Sundays before mass,
Lyric indulgences
Foretelling private tragedies.
College years, the apartment with the shag green carpet
On Ocean Avenue in Santa Cruz
Will forever harbor the 25-minute
Bellas Artes potpourri concert version of "Hasta que te conocí."
Your voice, flooding speakers in gay bars in San Francisco,
Los Angeles, Buenos Aires, Tijuana, San Diego,
Mexico City…another generation
Will dance, and another and another,
Until there is no trace of who we were—only then
Will your voice disappear…

You ascend the heights of national glory, Oh pure *largesse*!
Angels, those androgynous sluts, await your arrival.
Clouds big as air balloons are mariachis
Playing instruments of unworldly light.
No one will judge you. God will not judge you.
Catholic Mexico never judged you.

God will restore your exalted Ciudad Juárez,
The Ciudad Juárez that is not a graveyard.
And you will again be the Juan Gabriel of the 1970s,
The cute *cachetón* with the sensual Mexican lips,
And the sad eyes.

We will be who we have always been.
We will sing your songs…
We forgive the bad acting and the forgettable movies,
The sincerity of sentimentality.
It was always about the music,
About love—what we could or could not have,
But felt and lived nonetheless,
In those sublime hells of the heart,
The high notes of torment.

Lovelessness, distorted hearts, passion,
Tainted by your songs
Plunged us into the *cursi*.
But we couldn't stop. No, thank God
We couldn't stop ourselves.
Our Mexican lives, cauldrons of contradictions,
Nights of drunkenness and madness,
Your songs redeemed.

You are carrying 1,500 songs
To place at the feet of the Virgen de Guadalupe, or María Félix.

We will make joy of our suffering, your singing insists.
Mariachis send us off when we die.
In the meantime, devalued coins
Replay you in the jukeboxes of survival.

The Sirens and Odysseus

Feminine island voices
Where ocean depths taught them
The dark reaches of silence
And the surf's turbulent conservatory
The superhuman pitch of what has never seen sky
Or breathed air

Legend has it
They have wings
An irresistible speech granted by flight
By the wind and the sea's violent distances

You who must wander a flightless gender
Tied to their isolated choir
Destined to hear your sister-Self multiplied

You were chosen for the dangers of song
To be glorious music's singular brother

Screen Memories

Sleep buries into the years
Digging up the disowned and traumatic.
Dreams are of enemies or lovers.

I dreamt of my first love again, the one I hardly
Ever think about, but that my dreams will not forget.
In a murky tropical landscape that never knew us, reunited,
We are hesitant, awkward, uncertain.

Another dream: an obscene nemesis, my archenemy,
A truly ugly person,
I partner in pornographic scenes.

I wake to the aftertaste of death.

The Painter Edvard Munch and the Peruvian Mummy at the Universal Exposition, Paris, 1889

Violent brushstrokes
     Figured away
The rooted   the consecrated
     Pale spiritless eyes
En masse gawked at

My royal death
     He looted
Ransacking tribal centuries
     Millenary rituals
To assign my immortality his own
     Gesture of fear

Removed from Andean land
     My exhibited afterlife
          Invaded by deforming colors

From a tomb attended by ancestral gods
     He extracted anguish
Claiming my divine stature
     His own right to terror

He called it a Scream
The unlawful imposing ogling

Brothers Grimm

*...but even while they pretend to be lost in their fairy-tale
they're steeped in their vision of the dead restored.*
—Henry James, *Turn of the Screw*

Over the centuries they scattered witches   ogres   monstrous parents
                    Princes   kings
        Depositing generations of children in the German forest

We have been hungry and abandoned
        Recipients of kisses and the magic of death

And here we are
        The cities and suburbs stretching before us
                Glittering and dark
                        Like the endlessness of forests

The Ancestors Remember Antonin Artaud

*"And a White, for these Red Men, is one whom the spirits
have abandoned…"*
—Artaud, "Voyage to the land of the Tarahumaras"

Ill-omened apparition
    Soiled Christ-like man
Walking the time-sculpted mountains
    The scorching seas of the Sierra's sands

    On ancient rock formations
Inscribed he saw   the signs of gods
    The soul's hieroglyphs

Convinced our Peyote rite
    Held salvation
    A release from
Imprisoning white-haunted deadness

Prophecy's native son
    He was also its enemy

And as he arrived   he left
    Elsewhere   to remember us

Chapala in Early August

A day to read Vallejo, nothing more.
       The lake under an ancient spell,
Blessed and mild the rhythmic glare of its waters,
       But nothing in relation to my soul.
Forgive me, daylight perfection, for being so neglectful!

I want to be alone, although it hurts
       To the bottom of my childhood.

The world distances itself, takes
       Humanity along.
It is not self-pity
       To think that love and tenderness
Have been orphaned. That poets are the
Capricious children of the world's wounded parents—

But who are they, the progenitors
       Who didn't make a place
       For us in our skin, in their love, in those
             Warring political parties of the spirit?

Parental figures: All those lovers
Who couldn't love or only feigned affection,
       Punishing figures
           Of nocturnal hours.
An evil leak in the vessels of lineages
       Made us descendants.

The hours of a beautiful day trickle along,
       And I look forward
To the night, its death song of indifference.

The pregnant night awaits in the holy dark lap of summer
Bloated with the immaculate conception of morning.
In foundling morning light
We'll again be born,
Deformed and beautiful,
Revered like ancient Maya.

Russia's Poets

The Russian poets lead
to cities of snow, Orthodox cathedrals,
      war and criminal intrigue.

In the City of Angels
the translated lyrics of a tragic land
      claim me a citizen.

I walk in sunshine, in the glare
of avoided movies, separation and betrayal.

And the turbulences of love
      are pure nostalgia.

Sebastian in the Encantadas

He thought it unfitting to ever take any action
about anything whatsoever!—except to go on doing
as something in him directed
         —Tennessee Williams, *Suddenly, Last Summer*

Drums beating to the collective
Racing breath of orgies
Rain a thunderous baptism of semen

In this island
Destined for my enchanted kind
For a poet to find

Let it be known
I offered the gift of my flesh
That my head
Be a crown on an elegant stake

Don't excavate my remains
Mnemosyne's body parts

I was delivered to God
Whose motherless bone-white face
I recognized
In the searing obliterating
Caribbean sun

My bones have grained into sand
Like diamond sequins flooring the night
Kindling the ocean's awesome clamoring pull
Its waters boiling with Christ's fish
Multiplying like my insatiable lust

Lessons

Like money underneath a mattress
The professor finishes another book,
Places it back on the bookcase.
Times of distrust and secret hoardings.
Affection, tenderness—scarce currencies.

All the young men he comes across,
Lonely, restless, unfulfilled,
Are his ghosts,
Enslaved to pleasure
Or incurably isolated.

Out in the city is the future,
The dislocation of what will happen.
Inside are the words
And the music of apartness—the past.
Memory is spending itself.

News from Stockholm

In another world Tranströmer has died.
It snows in other countries, in other lives.

When a poet dies he doesn't miss
The world, or only misses a few things:
Making love, the smiles of children, the ocean,
The moon, Haydn, the taste of mangos.

Still, he'll find their equivalent experiences
Where he's gone, far from us, in the presence of all we lack.

Tranströmer has died. It is raining in Sweden.
Here in the tropics of Central America, the
Pacific is colder than usual
As if the surf delivered waters originating in the North Sea.

Star Sightings

I have seen stars in Los Angeles
Leonardo di Caprio   Scarlett Johansson

Unlike mortals coming upon gods in Greek mythology
        Nothing transpired

        I have sighted porn stars too
        Pointed out by others
They have the daguerreotype eyes of John Brown
        Brilliantly empty
Teeming with otherworldly violence
        Underneath clothes
One knows their bodies
To be eternally stripped of private sanctity
Granted by profane violation
A sacred   or a slave aura
Inaccessible to the free
To you   and to me

But you realize   you too
Have been a porn actor
In rooms absent of cameras
Satisfied   or ashamed
Your remained pure   anonymous

Such is the ambrosia of fame
Its taste of adoration and distance

Loulou

*Since a long time the parrot had been on Félicité's
mind, because he came from America...When
clouds gathered on the horizon and the thunder
rumbled, Loulou would scream, perhaps because he
remembered the storms in his native forests.*
          —Gustave Flaubert, *A Simple Heart*

An out of place splendor
My feathers' tropical green,
Cochineal, gold and emerald.
Plundered fantasia of America,
I am the far away, the absolute foreign.
My jailers are the anti-Adam.
Everything they name they alienate.
Like Caliban, they taught me
Language, their idiocies.
The slavery they invented
Detains and preserves
My stuffed afterlife.

In marvelous taxidermized flight
I become the Holy Ghost
To Félicité, poor countrywoman
Enraptured by my origins.
She's the least mad
In this Cartesian country
Of my cold eternal exile.

The Times

The Metro Red Line to Hollywood at 7 in the morning
      Caffeine and resilience
          Commuter silence

      Hunched over on the train seat
A young man slumbers in a drugged dream
      The night still clings to him
          The hours of oblivion
      In the bowels of downtown

      His pale ravaged face
Is the face of Che after the Bolivian jungle

      He will sleep through many stops
Despair and movement
      Without destination

Thomas Mann in the Palisades

Afternoon walks. Palm trees, the sea breeze coming in.
Jacaranda, like ruby-colored waterfalls dousing newly-built walls.
Apollonian sun, sensual, innocent sunset, Mediterranean,
It brings back Tuscany, Egypt, Palestine.

Thwarted aging Dionysus. The waiter a child of his pent-up lust.
The man's young American eyes, they fall
Casually on the distinguished foreigner.

Faust is the fatherland, incest and secrets,
Crimes read between the pages of newsprint. The Jews.
Cries for help cable in from Marseilles, Vichy,
Perpignan, Casablanca, Portugal…
Seasonless warmth, the atonal breaking of waves on the shore,
And Hollywood, the celluloid New World,
A short drive down Sunset Boulevard.

The Pacific, avocado groves, coastal mountains,
Hints of the tropics, Old Testament patriarchs,
Abyss and allegory, a parody.

Long dinners, the émigré social scene, family life,
The European mind transplanted, continues.
But the waiter, his smile, his eyes,
The dangerous summoning of a father's lust for his son.

On the Amtrak Train

After Wasco, a young man released from one of the prisons
In the depressed towns between Bakersfield and Fresno
Asks to borrow my cell phone.
A brown carton in the seat next to his
Contains all that he owns.
He's a character escaped from a fairy tale
In which the forest has been replaced
By some inner city in the Southland.
He has the eyes of a scared child
In which innocence is running amok.
Three days later I get a call from an unrecognized number.
It's his brother, who didn't pick up his call.
The man's name, I find out, was Joe.

El fantasma de Pita Amor

Sus pestañas falsas son las alas de los pajaritos enanos
Grises angelitos diminutos, dueños de vuelos de ida y vuelta
En el Bosque de Chapultepec.

El ritmo de los tacones de putas que marchan sin éxito
Obran sonetos impotentes que los travestis interpretan
Al cantar boleros en antros que sudan cerveza cansada.

Los perros abandonados la ven, la huelen
Su perfume de un Paris pasado de moda,
Ladran poseídos por la vanidad rabiosa
Siguen sus pasos en las banquetas
El mapa de su antigua caminata
Que navegan para terminar en un coger de rabioso abandono.

Su casa es la ciudad, angustiada metrópolis que devora
La presencia embriagadora de dioses enterrados
Por los siglos de los siglos, Amen,
Amen a su nombre,
Amen a su leyenda exhausta que se niega a descansar.

Sueña en los cuernos de los toros asesinados después de la corrida.
Lleva florecitas marchitadas a las tumbas de toreros.

Las mariposas pintadas de azules y rojos
De su sombra de ojos
La acompañan, le bailan valses sobre su coronita chueca
Y por encima de las flores que adornan su cabellera.

Las gatas embarazadas la esperan
Ella es la curandera de los partos clandestinos
De los gatitos bebés que los echan al río
No llora por ellos, ni por sus fans, ni por su vida extinguida
En el mundo de carne y hueso y de deseos.

En las esquinas urbanas de la oscuridad
Reclama los reflejos de bellos cadáveres
Y de nostalgias mas allá del bien y del mal.

Ella callejea, y sus pasos relatan el cuento de hadas
Que es la ciudad, su casa enfermiza y encantada.

The Ghost of Pita Amor

Wings of midget sparrows are her false eyelashes
Gray angels flying round trip
In Chapultepec Park.

The rhythm of whore high-heels walking without success
Compose impotent sonnets that transvestites interpret
Singing boleros in bars that sweat tired beer.

Stray dogs see her, smell her
Perfume from an outdated Paris
Possessed by rabid vanity they bark
Follow her steps on the sidewalk
The map of her ancient trail
That they follow to a famished fuck.

The city is her house, anxious metropolis devouring
The drunken spell of buried gods
Now and forever, Amen,
Amen to her name,
Amen to her exhausted legend that refuses rest.

She dreams of the horns of murdered bulls after the bullfights,
Places wilted flowers on the tombs of toreros.

Eye shadow butterflies
In blues and reds
Accompany her, dance little valses under her broken tiara
And the stolen flowers that adorn her head are nectarless.

Pregnant cats await her
She is the midwife of secret births
Of kittens drowned in the river
She doesn't cry for them, or her fans, or for her former life
In a world of flesh and bone
And lust.

In dark urban corners
She reclaims the images of beautiful corpses
And nostalgias beyond good and evil.

She streetwalks, and her steps relate a fairy tale
City, her sick, enchanted house.

Translation by author

Mérida

For David Santos

Buried ruins, Mayan tropics,
Heat without end in a colonial city,
Heat without escape
Like lust in the grip of sex—
You will always be Mérida:
Fantasies and fears marooned
In an air-conditioned hotel room.
Confessions of strangers
Where the cooled air recalls
The chill inside provincial cathedrals.
The news of a beautiful 20-year-old boy
Murdered in a dark room in the *centro histórico*.
A poem by José Emilio Pacheco
And a poem by Vicente Quirarte
That foretold our encounter.

And yet, why this compulsion to love
The dark children of the Death Wish?
Now all the young men in Cernuda's poems are you,
The ghost of who I could have been
If in my youth there had not been a plague.

And so we found each other, in nights
Devoured by our parting.
Nothing fated survives.
But what could not continue strews its gifts
Across other bodies that will take our place.

Buenos Aires

Caged at the zoo
Borges' tiger skulks behind bars
Bored enraged

At the Evita Museum
Dior dresses and "pickaninny" dolls
Wait for her return

South American outpost
Paris' phantom limb
Europe's outer reaches
Mimesis most successfully realized
At the Recoleta cemetery

Psychoanalysis
Plastic surgery dreams
They do come true

One can believe in anything
Even falling in love
Or the glamour of poets committing suicide
Even the ghost of Che haunting
The soccer crotches of neurotic boys

City of immigrants
City of monuments
Rooted to the elsewhere of the world

Alejandra Pizarnik writes a poem
for Janis Joplin

Sing sweetly and die after
No
Macbeth's Weird Sisters agree

Inside every Buddhist
Is an aborted rock star
Trapped in luxury hotel rooms
Rock-and-Roll wants to destroy

Sing savagely and live after
No
Blake's angels agree
But then again
They are silent

Listen to them

Jorge Cuesta at the Threshold

Cybele's relentless grip
Is reconstructing me
Ousting the anatomical markers of manhood.
Philistine medical science is powerless
Before the ascendency of ancient gods.

My body is the *prima materia*
Of a future alchemy of genders:
James Bond girls, reality TV stars,
Hermaphrodite celebrities, intersex inner-city prostitutes,
Ladyboy call girls who specialize in refined tastes…
Yes, the victorious ones who overcome
All evidence of the virile.

But today, in 1942, my metamorphosis
Is curtailed. I am abandoned at the threshold.
Mutilation and Death impose their order:
To be stillborn in the engendering mirror of poetry,
Where man, woman and their limits are at war.

Hart Crane Leaves Mexico

The ocean's razor brilliance
        shimmers
    in the horizon's definitive promise

One final violence
      will I bequeath
to depths beyond the waves' surface chaos
      the sundering distances
of absolute lyrics

Foundling son of death's baptismal cadence
      I am become salt and bottomless obscurity
      seabed serenity
      where sailors' bones
awaken Christ in my soul-emptied skeleton
      as sharks ritually circle
to the calling of mute siren lullabies

Vagrant illuminations barricade Puritan shores
      boundless cold dissolution
        is my coming home

Pizarnik

La escena final es femenina, finamente elaborada,
A la altura de lo poético y lo *maudit*.

Es el teatro de la muerte,
El laboratorio de la fama.
Allí quedaron las muñecas maquilladas,
La nota legendaria,
El silencio y sus máscaras.

Hasta allí arrastraste la noche
La dejaste colgada
Entregada a las maravillas de Alicias fracasadas.

Fue el triunfo.

Luego llega el comercio y el kitsch
El folklore de la vida cotidiana

Y los militares,
La música clandestina de la tortura.

No te culpo, pero me avergüenza
Admitir que te creo…

Hay flores disfrazadas de azul en Buenos Aires,
Muertes que todavía te esperan,
Espejos embrujados por tu ausencia,

Y tus poemas—oscuros adioses—
En todas la ciudades.

Te permitiste todo.

Pizarnik

The final scene is feminine, shrewdly elaborate,
Poète maudit at its pinnacle.

It's the theatre of death,
Laboratory of fame,
Where you left dolls with make-up on,
The legendary note,
Silence and its masks.

Assailing the farthest reaches of night
You left darkness hanging
Surrendered to the wonderlands of failed Alices.

A triumph.

Then came the marketplace and kitsch
The folklore of the quotidian

Murderers
The clandestine music of torture.

I don't blame you, but I'm embarrassed
To admit I believe you…

Flowers costumed in blue in Buenos Aires,
Death still awaiting your arrival,
Mirrors bewitched by your absence,

And your poems—dark adieus—
In all the cities.

You permitted everything.

Translation by author

Suburban Cemetery

Scenic Cemetery on Scenic Avenue, is where
The Mexicans who die now
Neighbor the sons and daughters
Of Gold Rush pioneers.
Forever they keep company
With the timeless silence of stone angel statues,
The marble Madonnas with devotional blank stares,
Their otherworldly, uninterrupted vigils,
In tended acres of green-lawned grasses
And sad flowers,
Fresh with the commemoration of loss.

Across Scenic Avenue, facing the cemetery
The public psychiatric ward
Safeguards nightmares and screams.

I imagine the mad steal furtive looks at the cemetery
From the latticed windows that hide them
To see hovering over the headstones
The wings of angels at rest after flight
Their untarnished beauty-queen faces
Poised above tombstones whose worn whiteness
Reminds the confined
Of life on the outside, it's bright pleasures
Its intoxications, its dangers.

Angelic haze of January sunshine.
Scenic Cemetery is a garden where peace
Blooms and sorrow is tranquilized forever.
I see, from a distance, fragments of anonymous angels

The graceful poses of sun-bleached Madonnas
Who wouldn't exist without the dead
Who were not made to pray
For the insane, for the living.

Forgettable Monsters

My friend Berta sold Cuban cigars on the black market
when we were students in San Diego.
> Changó and Yemanyá travel with her,
> she observes necessary rituals.

My friend tells that in the 1980s
Fidel Castro created genetically altered fish
> and chicken hybrids,
mutant meat for human consumption.

The creatures could fly from the rivers
> up into the trees.
and kept the Cuban people from starving.

> Unrealizable ambition
or madness?
> Far from utopias and tropics,
> we too
feed on forgettable monsters.

An Anthology of 20th Century
Argentinian Poetry, 1981

printed when the generals ruled
and poets   the lyrical
told terror   told it slant

Borges made his appearance
was it before
or after his praising of the "gentlemen"
bringing order to the country?
Alejandra Pizarnik unfazed unmoved
plucked flowers of evil
from her torment-tended garden
Olga Orozco reported on the horoscope
and wrote odes to Berenice her regal cat
who communicated from the feline afterlife

for Jacobo Fijman in the insane asylum
          nothing changed
God did not change   agony did not alter
I don't recall if Juan Gelman and Julio Cortázar
          were absent
from the table of contents
          why don't I remember?

bought from a street kiosk in Buenos Aries
for years its pages kept more innocent company
in the masses of my bookcases

but the book's lack of innocence
became more pronounced
the homeliness of evil tinted

the cheap beige paper
its nondescript imageless cover
its sad guilty colorlessness

I donated it to my neighborhood bookstore

but time makes curiosity a dark longing
          and the dreams
crimes   occult signs
          of the anthologized poets
          beckon me
imprisoned sirens in the lyre's concentration camp

they sing of abandonment
that they are not guilty
that they didn't know
that it was not cynicism or opportunism

that I will never hear from them again

Thin White Duke

A Mexican boy, like so many
Taken from Planet Pueblo, a Michoacán universe
Unvisited by narcos and drug wars
During the fall of the American Empire no one took notice of.

Creatures of dislocation we were, paying for the sins
Of history's occlusions.

La Llorona came first, and the story my *primas* told:
A giant fish chained up inside a church
Atop a nearby mountain
Was Christ's freak gift.
The divine fish was made of gold,
With diamond eyes big as boulders.
When it broke loose in a God-inspired earthquake,
It shattered upon the town more gold and diamonds
Than the townspeople knew what to do with…

Then came Ziggy Stardust, apparition
On the late-night TV screen, landed in the middle
Of the 1970's, great crater between
Hippies and disco.

A child uprooted from Edenic Mexico, moon-
Walking the lunar emptiness of California's suburbs,
Abandoned to the incomprehensible, disorienting worlds of
The English language, football and baloney sandwiches, who
Recognized in him/her/it —
What would take him out of the known
To the borders of understanding.

All I know is that a church in Coalcomán houses an elegant
Life-size statue of Christ in a glass case;
Believers cross themselves, touch the glass in reverence
As they solemnly march past.

The Nazarene's refined, gaunt plaster face
Is both foreign and familiar, ethereal.
It is the face of David Bowie, but bloodied, destined for Mexico.
His wounded body marked by colonial centuries
Under a sexual spell that refuses
To be named.

Mexican Christ, Thin White Duke,
Patron Saints
Of dolls queer boys played with in secret shame,
Patron saints too of outcast daydreams,
Of the pixies of masturbation,
Of white cholas with raccoon eyes in the Airport district in Modesto,
Of the science fiction of tears from the galaxies of lust and love,
Of deranging music composing our lives…

David Bowie, good wizard,
The fairy dust you sprinkled on childhood
Is finally settling.
We are tarnished gold, rejected rhinestone, exiled silver,
Psychedelic glitter, outdated colors, tinsel,
Cancer, illness, madness, alcoholism, recovery, survival, art, poetry…

Some of us are finding God.
We are stardust in an alien night.

MYSTERY PLAYS: A BLUEBEARD CYCLE

If monstrosity was recognizable you would see it and maybe you would avoid it, but most of the time monstrosity is not recognizable, it's just a mask of normality.

—Isabelle Huppert

Where is the stage: outside or within,
Ladies and gentlemen?

—Prologue, Duke Bluebeard's Castle Libretto
by Béla Balázs

Disfigurement

The dead in me resisted

The dead—
Faithful to truth, a collective story

I was bequeathed
A dismembered fairy tale:

The violated, conquered past.

Brother Bluebeard

I.

Secret lover of mirrors,
Narcissus you had let drown.
Furtively used looking glasses
Stood transfixed in the empty
Magic of power.

II.

Sure sentiments died upon arrival.
The castle was in the throes
Of the music you composed,
The gardens you tended.

Prying me open,
You enflamed curiosity
And simultaneously made it an offense.
You confessed the trials of insufferable women
Who wanted to know too much.
I thought they had nothing to do with me;
Being a man, I didn't need to know, only to have.

Co-conspirator, partner in crime,
I delivered myself to unintelligible restrictions,
Not realizing this was the path
To the darkest recesses of the castle,
From which women
Had never returned.

III.

Houseplants thrived.
Mourning and grief did not.
You did not tolerate ghosts of any kind.

IV.

I embraced the rage of your withholdings, your caginess,
The disarming invitations of your praises,
And irresistibly treaded, exploring all the rooms.
The trackless cold pinnacles of sex
Opened upon the secret dead:
Corpses like letters spelling your true name.

V.

I had dreams that I was fucking women.
Did your dead haunt my dreams?
"I knew you were like me," you said.
And unlocked the secret chamber:
The deep intimate cavern
Of tortures, humiliations, derangements,
Shining like your soul's hoarded jewels,
Blindingly apart.
I thought Romantic isolation would unite us,
But the dread I tried to circumvent
Told otherwise.

VI.

I belonged to the dead
During my time in the castle,
Feeling your equal
Even as my sisters hung like pheasants
Below the floors where we dined, fucked
And read Borges and Baudelaire.
I refused to hear the slow, steady
Dripping of their blood.
It was the music of my future.

VII.

You said, "You are like me."
Meaning not like the others, the men—
Superficial, frivolous, uninteresting.
"You could never be with one of them,
They would bore you to death."
I gave myself to your claim,
With misguided pride, in the abasement
That inspired you.

Oh, brotherhood of one, brother Bluebeard,
Those men you didn't have to murder
Because they didn't aim to understand.
In the nameless sex you had with them
And that they have with each other,
You are annihilated.
Every ecstatic breath they share
Extinguishes all traces of you.

VIII.

I thought cum was a clandestine potion, an amulet,
That would bring security,
Ushering in, through the back door, permanency.
I didn't realize I had surrendered,
Until I felt my blood course in your voice.
The cold winds of truth entered the castle
And I found myself prisoner.
The spell was broken,
I knew I had been betrayed,
By me, by you.

IX.

When I think of you now, I see myself, a stranger,
Adrift amidst isolated mirrors.
How did your Peer Gynt seductions succeed?
Terror, tenderness, what was it that entrapped me?

Vain explorer, witness, survivor,
I inherited the memory of the dead,
The unmarked graves of love.

The Grooming

You knew the score
the finale that would
reveal it all   as premeditated:

the bi-coastal trips   the Los Angeles reprieves
long distance secrets
Oh, master of closed doors!

colorless cannibal
banqueting on
the hunger of others

Seduction

Come to the snow country
You said, not with words, but with affectionate gestures,
Come to picturesque New England where
Deformed apples grow
Deformed because Nature is not interfered with.

You came bearing gifts, like the Tarot's Magician,
A lover offering personalized specialties.

Oh, walk with me where the deer hunters
Are given permission to hunt on my property.
You do, and do not, want
To see the hunters carrying the dead deers,
The meat I share with their killers
A delicacy I will prepare for you.
Death is the spice of seduction
Indeed, *mon cher*, hesitancy and ambiguity
An added attraction.
I offer it all to you, a gift, it is me.
You are fascinated, you should be.
There were Others, but they did not kiss like you,
I've never kissed anyone like I do you…
Do not mind the way
I've disposed of the countless before you.
All this is a feast to take in
And you will never know it
Unless you let me prepare it, display it.
Take my hand, my dear,
Walk my grounds,
Help me with my garden, listen to my music,
I will climb with you the nearby mountains.

You love being a guest, but you are more than a guest,
You are my latest, most deserving guest.
And yes, this is a big inherited house, a castle of sorts,
Populated by death, but teeming to the brim
With exuberance.
Do not notice the shadows, the neglected sorrow
That follows you up the steps
Or the pools of silver silence, the mirrors,
Wherein are buried screams
Withdrawn and never heard from again.
Do not give it a moment's notice
The times I look away in absence and distance.
Something else lures me,
Something that puzzles you,
Something I'm orchestrating
In the cold caverns
Of my heartless body.

Composer

Staccato notations
Controlling cacophony!

Every note was a laceration
Exacting torrents of torment.

Music, my ally,
Betrayed you.

On the page, the symphony score:
Derivative Dvořák, banal imitations of Bartók
Strident screechings striving after Stravinsky.

The music knew what I did not.

Conversion

Your body— structure of confinement—
        I tried to make a home.

        Fiefdom of feminine death—
Always there were presences, apparitions,
        That would not let peace be.

I acquiesced, but the collusion of the conquered,
Looking the other way, like a bystander,
        Allowed your lineage to continue

While you counted and calculated
        Traceless bodies accumulated.

The Eternal Feminine

Buffoon criminal, hapless Bluebeard
mudding up Narcissus' waters
gorging on the shattered reflections
            of others.

            What was my crime?
the crime of every woman:

Loving a mediocre artist,
            a basic, dreary man.

Settler Colonialism

Destruction's favored child
threatened by all that was whole and benign

      Oh Judas, Iago,
            Bluebeard bloodline
                  madly coursing
through the prisons of cities
      the neverlands of hope

Conquistador

Swineherd   armed wooer
     Soldier
     Of glass trinket affections

Seducer of Russian brides   Chinese brides
     Filipino Brides
So easy to deceive   to detain

     Rainbow coalition of brides
Entrenched from generation to generation
     To your claims   your pillaging

The brides were never annihilated

     They called you home

A Prayer to the Brides

Forgive me
Sisters of a sad shared pedigree
Lifeline of subjugation

Pray for me
In centuries of forgetfulness
From the abyss of the mapless

Feminine family tree
Ruled by the constancy of treachery
Do not forsake me!
I renounce all Bluebeardy brotherhoods!

Oh, conflicted bitchery
Patriarchy's colluder
Foolish sisters   do not
Root me to your family tree!

Survivor's Guilt

Dead brides unionized their haunting—
      Macbeth's Weird Sisters
or bipolar muses drunk as maenads?

Mistresses of nerves,
           feminine, determined,
      shackled me to wanting,
           to inescapable longing.

I didn't know it was war
      I had walked into.

      I overlooked
the dead behind the door—
      los desaparecidos.

BALLADS OF INNER LIFE,
OR THE END OF BLUEBEARD

Porque del gran delito de quererte
Sólo es bastante pena confesarlo.

Of the grand crime of loving you
It's painful enough to confess it.

—Sor Juana Inés de la Cruz

Wound for red wound I burn to smite their wrongs;
And there is absolution in my songs.

—Siegfried Sassoon

Demon Lover

Wounded bird, pleasure's predator

Loyal only to despoiling,
to bottom dwelling carrion— your element.

Refused by human heights,
only the groundless night knew you.

Romantic Landscape

You led me on a beautiful Connecticut spring day
      To a field of daffodils

But the part did not become you
      Between you and a season in blossom
Roused the absence of communion:
      Wordsworth was dead
          Transcendence a travesty

Pinnacles you put before me:
      Unconvincing flowers

Beauty belittled by your claims

      Nature would not let you enter
Father yourself into her

Your lips were not made to cure sadness

Now it all makes sense
I read in a line of Alfonsina Storni
"Tus labios no se hicieron para curar tristeza."
Those thin lips— slight, emptied of memory,
       Impostors of sensuality.
I can't say they stirred up passion or that I
Longed for them, even at the height of…
And though we laughed together
       I don't recall the laughter
Such a miserly mouth voiced.

Lips of men incapable of surrender,
Whose bodies are instruments.
Men who wound greedily
And without conviction, love nothing,
And leave sadder any sorrow that they touch.

Omens

       For years
birds met me in my wanderings
         crows   hawks
pelicans screeching in swarms   hunting violent shores
dead blue jays underneath L.A. freeway overpasses

       Birds enraged   maimed   beheaded
struggling omens of injury and flight
         following our bond to its conclusion

       And at high noon
       from an 8th floor window
       in the most urban part of the city
the ritual visit of a hummingbird
bearing the occult nectar of healing…

It was distortion
       that let you in

       True music
is a translation
       of nature's revenge

Revolution

Plagued by alienation and doubt
I didn't realize we, bride brotherhood,
The murdered and the living,
      Shared the key

To the dark chamber, the last
      Hold out of tyranny.

The forbidden room
      Was always ours.

Displaced children
Will storm your castle

      And it will be theirs.

Thanatos

Soul mate of the Death Instinct

With your nerves
The murdered conducted
Symphonies of agony
Secret songs of solidarity

Your delirious vanity
Gave them standing ovations

City of Angels

Bicycling in the city
I came upon a dying cowbird
        splattered on dark concrete
        bloodied wings fluttering in anguish
the final release of life's flight

        I cycled away
sensed the demons of attachment
        dissipating
in the smoggy soiled
        light of sunset

I stopped being a prisoner

Bluebeard's Gift

Your key— instrument of death.
Your key—a gift.

Behind the final door
The blood murals of erasure
Where phantom figures
Etched you into shadow.

I locked you in. And turned the key
Forever on your rule.

Your screams revived
Stifled harem terrors
The furies of communal horror.

Cryptic room devoid of mirrors
Gallery of imageless internment
Wedded to the lowest rung of abandonment.

The brides became you.
Duplicated brides encircle you
In prayerless eternity.

Bluebeard's Gravestone

What remains of barbaric white noise
Orchestrated to invoke passion, enthusiasm,
Perplexing noisemaking optimal for seduction?

Where neither art or nature
        Placed you
You intervened, imposed your supremacy
Mining the deepest recesses of unwarranted loving.

In the end, the unraveled notes of false melodies
        Revealed your most lasting score:

        An unmourned death
 An unvisited grave in Connecticut
        Unattended
        Even the snow
Covering your name
        Doesn't get used to the letters.

The flowers and the years were relieved
        The unrecorded justice of the dead
Inspired birds to soar and to sing

        Undefeated by femicide.

Notes

Juan Gabriel (1950-2016) is the most significant popular singer in Mexican musical history. An innovative, prolific songwriter and composer, his music transcends Mexican popular music genres and continues to appeal to Mexicans of every generation. In a heteronormative, Catholic society, Juan Gabriel nonetheless was permitted to be himself—queer, flamboyant and free. Juan Gabriel was born in Ciudad Juárez, where he lived his adolescence, and where he began his singing career in the local bars of this border city. The word *cursi* is a nuanced word, it encompasses a combination of the sappy, the corny and the affected.

Art Historians have speculated that Edvard Munch's famous painting "The Scream" was inspired by a Peruvian mummy, buried with its hands clutching its face, which was exhibited in the Universal Exhibition in Paris in 1889.

Antonin Artaud traveled to Mexico in 1936. Upon his return to France the following year he was committed to psychiatric institutions until his death in 1948.

Physical deformities in Mesoamerican civilizations were considered divine attributes granted to humans by the gods.

Sebastian Venable is a character in Tennessee Williams' *Suddenly, Last Summer.* He does not appear in the play, but his presence haunts the drama as a whole. Sebastian, a young queer poet, has been killed by cannibal natives in the fictional island of the Encantadas.

Loulou is a parrot in Gustave Flaubert's short story "A Simple Heart." Loulou is acquired by Félicité, a servant in Normandy who comes to believe taxidermized Loulou is a manifestation of the Holy Spirit.

Guadalupe Teresa Amor Schmidtlein (1918-2000), better known as Pita Amor, was a poet of aristocratic origins. Her book of poems *Yo soy mi casa* (1946) (*I Am my House*) was dedicated to her friend Gabriela Mistral, the Chilean Nobel prize laureate. An extravagant, scandalous beauty, she was painted by Diego Rivera, Raul Anguiano and Juan Soriano. In her later years she became a hermit, arrogant, rude and eccentric, a sort of troll poetess. Alfonso Reyes, Mexico's most significant literary figure of the 20th century stated, "...with Pita we are talking about a mythological phenomenon."

Alejandra Pizarnik (1936-1972) Argentine poet of dark Romantic themes in the tradition of Baudelaire, Nerval and Rimbaud. Considered one of the most significant Latin American poets of her generation. She committed suicide in Buenos Aires in 1972. Pizarnik wrote a poem about Janis Joplin after the North American singer's death.

Jorge Cuesta (1904-1942) One of the most influential and enigmatic of Mexican modern poets. He was a member of Los Contemporáneos, a group of predominantly queer, vanguard poets and critics whose interests were cosmopolitan, experimental and modernist. After a mental breakdown and a horrific act of self-castration, he was interned in a psychiatric hospital in Tlalpan where he committed suicide.

Hart Crane committed suicide by jumping from a U.S. bound ship in the Gulf of Mexico in 1932.

Bluebeard, in this reconfiguring of the tale, has a modern profession— he is a composer of classical music, an artist of sorts, a failed artist. The sources for Bluebeard poems are the classic folk tale by Charles Perrault and Bela Bartok's opera "Duke Bluebeard's Castle." In Béla Balázs' libretto for

"Duke Bluebeards's Castle" the castle represents Bluebeard's body and his inner life.

The section titled "Mystery Plays" references the Mystery Play, a theatrical genre from the Middle Ages.

Bruno Bettelheim, in his classic psychoanalytic study of the fairy tale, *The Uses of Enchantment: The Meaning and Importance of Fairy Tales*, claims that "Bluebeard" "is not a fairy tale, because with the single exception of the indelible blood on the key which gives away the fact that Bluebeard's bride has entered the forbidden room, there is nothing magical or supernatural in the story." The bird motif in these Bluebeard poems is not strictly a "supernatural" element, but a symbolic representation of the characters' inner lives.

"Survivor's Guilt" ends with a reference to the disappeared, *los desaparecidos,* victims of torture, murder and disappearance in Latin American right-wing dictatorships in the 20th century.

Acknowledgments

Grateful acknowledgment is made to the editors of the following publications where these poems, sometimes in slightly different form, first appeared:

"Brother Bluebeard" "Conversion" "The Eternal Feminine" "Conquistador" "Survivor's Guilt" "Displacement" and "Revolution" in *Psychological Perspectives: A Quarterly Journal of Jungian Thought*

"Juan Gabriel Ascends to Heaven" in *Angel City Review: Ten Years of Poetry in LA*

"Loulou" and "An Anthology of 20th Century Argentinian Poetry" in *Plume.*

"The White Duke" in *Faultline: Journal of Art and Letters*

"Jorge Cuesta at the Threshold" "Screen Memories" and "Alejandra Pizarnik Writes a Poem for Janis Joplin" in *circulo de poesía*, translated by Andrea Rivas.

"Madame Neurosis" and "Narcissus Sleeping" in *Ducts*

"The Times" "Forgettable Monsters" and "Brothers Grimm" in *A Poetry Congeries*

"News from Stockholm" "Lessons" "Buenos Aires" "On the Train" in *Springhouse Journal*

"Chapala in Early August" in *Gulf Coast: A Journal of Literature and Fine Arts*

"The Sirens an Odysseus," published as "The Sirens" in *Plume 10 Anthology*

"Suburban Cemetery" in *Bitter Oleander Review*

My gratitude to Theresia de Vroom, founder and publisher of Walton Well press, for her vision and commitment. Many thanks to Gail Wronsky for poetry, for inspiration and her editorial support. Thank you to ash good for the design of this Walton Well book. I thank Elena Karina Byrne for help with the evolution of the poems and the structure of the book. And with gratitude to the poets, artists and friends who keep the light: Caroline LeDuc, David Garza, Samera Owhadian, Barbara Carrasco, Roberto Tejada, Francesco Siqueiros, Anthony Seidman, Nylsa Martínez, Harry Gamboa Jr., Sesshu Foster, Karen Kevorkian, Ruben Mendoza, Munia Bhaumik, Quentin Ring, Terese Svoboda, Chuck Rosenthal, Yreina Cervantez, Roberto Gil de Montes, Eddie Dominguez, Susan Silton, Vincent Ramos, Sandra de la Loza, Victoria Delgadillo, Raul Baltazar, Danny Lawless, Terry Wolverton, Margaret García, Susana Chávez-Silverman, Anjelina Sáenz, Steven Reigns, Ilana Dunn Luna, Gaspar Orozco Rios, Carolie Parker, Iván Salinas, Andrew Sapienza, Chloe Karina Sapienza, Suyapa Portillo, Alicia Partnoy, Antonio Leiva, Richard McDowell, Pablo Capra, Ruth Simard, Marc Simard, Lino Perez, Camille Norton, Mary Pardo, Stella Beratlis, Gloria Alvarez, Maggie Messerschmidt, Carribean Fragoza, Romeo Guzmán, Beatriz Cortez, Berta Jottar, Zachary Jensen, Ata Moharreri, Mariano Zaro, Molly Bendall, David Lloyd, Espie Valverde, Noel Alumit, Juana Mora and Rudy Acuña.

About the Author

Ramón García is the author of *The Chronicles* (Red Hen Press, 2015) and *Other Countries* (What Books Press, 2010), a monograph on the artist Ricardo Valverde (University of Minnesota Press, 2013) and a chapbook *Strays* (Foundlings Press, 2021).

His poetry has appeared in a variety of journals and anthologies, including *circulo de poesía, the Best American Poetry* anthology, *Poetry Goes to the Movies, The Los Angeles Review of Books* (LARB), *Mandorla: New Writing from the Americas, Gulf Coast* and *Plume*. A former Vice-President of the Board of Trustees at Beyond Baroque Literary Center in Venice, California, he is Associate Editor of *Plume* poetry magazine. He teaches at California State University, Northridge and lives in Los Angeles. HTTPS://RAMONGARCIAPHD.COM/